Resolve to Succeed

How to crack the New Year's Resolution

Josie Baxter.

Copyright © Josie Baxter 2016
All rights reserved world wide
No part of 'Resolve to Succeed – How to Crack the New Year's Resolution' may be reproduced or stored by any means without the express permission of Josie Baxter

Whilst reasonable care is taken to ensure the accuracy of the information in this publication, no responsibility can be accepted for the consequences of any actions based on any opinions, information or advice found in the publication.

ISBN-13: 978-1541139893

Also by Josie Baxter

How to Be Happy

Contents

Introduction	9
What is a resolution?	13
The history of New Year	15
The benefits of resolutions.	18
Some common pitfalls	20
Why resolutions fail	24
Types of New Year's resolution.	28
Setting a goal	33
Making your resolution a goal.	36
How to set a successful goal.	39
Creating life goals.	43
Tracking your success.	48
Create new habits.	52
Don't get distracted.	55
Declare your intentions.	60
Being accountable.	63
Have an accountability partner.	66
Benefits of accountability.	69

Create an action plan 73
Create deadlines. 74
Announce your goals. 75
An accountability partner. 76
Allow the unexpected. 76
Use tools to help you. 77
Visualisation. 78
Consequences. 79
Groups and forums. 80
Challenges. 80
Bite-size pieces. 81
Have a day off. 82
Take a break. 83
Success breeds success. 83
Keep a Journal. 84
Plan to succeed. 85
Set monthly goals. 85
Have self-belief. 86
Using affirmations. 86
Ask for help. 88
Setting milestones. 89
Resolution ideas. 95
Health and fitness. 95

Personal finance. 96

Career plans..96

Improve your skills. 97

Family goals. 97

Relationship goals...97

Introduction

We all start on 1st January with our New Year's resolution or maybe even our list of New Year's resolutions, but how often do you write that list, knowing full well that you won't achieve them.

Even when you start with the best of intentions and fully intend to follow through on your new year's resolutions, the unfortunate truth is that many of them will be long forgotten by 1st February.

It has become a habit that is destined to be a let-down, making unattainable resolutions that start in hope and end in exasperation and failure.

The fact that you have picked up this book means that you want to change that cycle in your life.

And this is the year to make that change. To make New Year's resolutions that will succeed.

The thing is, that in any part of life, a goal without a plan is just a wish. And most of us make that list of New Year's resolutions without any plan in place at all.

You're making a good start by searching out and then hopefully reading this book.

It is important to read it.

It's not just enough to have bought it and have it sitting on your shelf. That's the path of many a New Year's resolution, but if you want them to succeed you have to plan and you have to work at it and think how much better you will feel this time next year.

A large part of the path to success is to learn why you - indeed anyone - fails. If you understand the reason for failure you can avoid those pitfalls and you are much more likely to work through the problems and to succeed.

One of the wonderful things is that success breeds success. The more you succeed the more you are encouraged to work to continue your success. And success becomes a habit, a habit that can entirely transform your life.

So out with the old and in with the new.

A New Year, a new successful resolution, a new you.

The New Year's resolution

Josie Baxter

What is a resolution?

We make our list of resolutions at the end of every year, possibly far too close to the end of every year, in the midst of the party celebrations, when your mind isn't necessarily as clear as it should be.

But what is a resolution?

A resolution is basically a promise you make to yourself to do something good or to break a bad habit.

Of course, resolutions are not limited to the New Year, you can make one at any time and normally they are made at a time of change. This is of course the reason that the New Year is such a popular time for resolutions. After all it's a New Year, a new start, a new beginning. A chance to wipe out the mistakes and bad habits of the past.

But there can be lots of new starts.

It might be the end of the educational year and the start of a new life outside education.

It might be a time when you move to a new house or a new city, even a new state or country.

It could be the end of an old relationship and beginning of a new independent you.

Many things can prompt you to make a list of resolutions, things you will start doing, things you will stop doing, and the advice in this book can help you at any time that you decide to make a new resolution.

As the poet, Edith Lovejoy Pearce said

We will open the book, its pages are blank. We are going to put words on them ourselves. The book is called opportunity and its first chapter is New Year's Day.

The history of New Year

Celebrating New Year isn't something that has just happened recently. Many ancient peoples celebrated the New Year although not all of them in January. The Babylonians celebrated in March and the early Roman Empire followed this pattern. Celebrations around the time of the vernal equinox in mid-March were held in many ancient civilisations while others such as the Egyptians and Persians began their year with the fall equinox in mid-September and the Greeks celebrated the winter solstice in mid-December. These dates are for the northern hemisphere and follow the seasons of the year rather than a specific date

It wasn't until the Roman Emperor decided to completely overhaul the traditional Roman calendar in 45 BC and copy the Egyptian pattern that we ended up with the Julian calendar.

This wasn't a perfect calculation and over the course of a thousand years an error of seven days had slipped into the calendar. This was eventually corrected in 1582 when the Gregorian calendar was introduced giving us an extra day every four years, in the leap year and a celebration on 1st January to introduce each New Year.

The name of the month of January comes from the name of the God Janus, the Roman two faced God of beginnings and transitions, who possesses an ability to see the past and the future. He is also seen as the god of gates doorways and doors.

So, within the Roman world, which of course covered most of northern Europe and North Africa, January 1st became observed as the start of the New Year and the new calendar.

But our traditional celebration of New Year on 1st January actually isn't that traditional. In mediaeval Europe, celebrations were considered pagan and unchristian like and the Council of Tours even abolished January 1st as the beginning of the year in 567.

Sometimes New Year was celebrated on December 25th, March 1st or later in March - all Christian feasts of course. The birth of Jesus on Christmas day, the feast of the Annunciation and Easter, the start of the Christian year.

When the Gregorian calendar was introduced in 1582 it was adopted almost immediately in most Catholic countries, but only gradually in Protestant countries. For instance, in Britain it wasn't adopted until the mid-1700s, changing the traditional New Year celebration in March to January across the British Empire and America.

Although we have become used to celebrating New Year on 1st January throughout most of the Western world, it's also important to remember that other cultures have different New Year's. For instance the Chinese New Year, often known as the spring festival is celebrated on the new moon between 21st January and 20th February.

The Islamic lunar year is 11 to 12 days shorter than the Gregorian year, which means that the Islamic New Year varies every year, for example the Islamic year started on 29th December 2008 according to the Gregorian calendar but on 3rd October in 2016.

However and whenever you decide to celebrate your New Year, I hope that the rest of this book will help you to make meaningful New Year's resolutions and will help you keep to them and be successful in reaching your goals.

The benefits of resolutions.

So it's New Year, why should you make New Year resolutions?

After all you can make a resolution at any time, prompted by any reason or any event. But the fact is that most of us understandably see New Year as a chance to make a new start.

It's that first day on the first month of the New Year. Putting up a new calendar, opening a new diary, seeing another year start again.

It feels fresh. It feels new. It feels like a good time to start creating a new you.

And that's as good a reason as any.

A New Year's resolution can motivate you into taking the action you know you should have been taking all along.

We all have things in our life that we would like to change or improve. Some of them are very big things whereas others will be quite minor, and a New Year always feels like a good time to wipe the slate clean and start again.

When you make New Year's resolutions you feel like you are taking control of your life and making a decision to make the changes you need. This can be very powerful and it can help you get your life back on track, or move on from the situation you know is bad for you. It can make you take stock of your life, actually facing what is wrong or what could be better.

Many people decide to give up a bad habit such as smoking, eating too much chocolate or spending too much time in front of the TV. Other resolutions can be more active, a very popular one is to join a gym and get fit and unfortunately this is one of the resolutions that rarely makes it past the end of January.

When you do set a resolution that really means something to you personally, you have a much better chance of actually following through.

It always helps if you start out with confidence and determination, seeing your resolutions clearly, rather than through the hangover of the New Year's Eve party.

Setting and achieving Resolutions can improve your self-confidence and power your self-esteem. It will give you a wonderful sense of achievement when you see yourself succeeding, it can help bring back your pride in yourself, your abilities, and your belief that you can improve your life.

Some common pitfalls

So now we've seen the benefits of the New Year's resolution, how it can be powerful and motivational, but it can also be the opposite, dis-incentivising and bringing of sense of failure when you do not follow through on your New Year's resolution.

The thing is, so many of us set these New Year's resolution in the wrong frame of mind. If you fail to really think it through and just go for the same resolution year after year, which means failure after failure, you're setting yourself up for yet another failure. And each time that happens you will lose more confidence.

This happens when you pick the standard list of resolutions that you see in any magazine.

I will give up smoking.

I will lose weight.

I will get fitter.

These are by their very nature standardised, they not specific to you. This means you haven't really thought about it and you haven't really set your mind to something that you want in your life rather than just copying the pages of a magazine and following fashion.

You need to make your resolutions much more specific, more thoughtful and much more personal to you.

For instance, if you have decided that you are going to lose weight you need to really think about what that means to you and to your life. You need to set yourself a specific target and a specific plan. This needs a lot more thoughtful soul-searching than a simple quip at the New Year's Eve party.

Whatever your resolution is, you need to think clearly and deeply about it to see how you genuinely feel about the target you're setting yourself.

And you need to set a definite target. It's not enough to say I will lose weight, you need to set a proper plan.

I will lose 10 pounds by March 1st.

I will fit into my skinny jeans for the summer holiday.

I will have a six pack by Easter

When you start to do make a plan and set a target, when you are honest with yourself and think seriously about the changes you want to make in your life, it can bring up some very deep emotions. After all, you are doing some soul searching and looking clearly and coldly at what is wrong in your life. We often hide from these uncomfortable truths and live in a state of denial, but that won't help you to change anything.

When you actually deal with these deeper parts of yourself rather than simply following a fashion, the latest idea trending on social media or being influenced by peer pressure - in other words being shallow - you will give yourself a much greater chance of making real changes to your life.

A successful resolution really has to mean something to you. And it has to really mean something to you, not to somebody else who was pressurising you to make these changes. After all, only you know what you want genuinely, and only you can be in control of making the changes to give you that self-esteem and self-confidence.

Going on a diet, starting an exercise regime, cutting out alcohol or paying off your debts because someone else tells that you should, will never last because the desire and determination hasn't come from deep inside yourself.

So instead of making your list of New Year's resolutions in a rush on a scrap of paper on New Year's Eve, set aside some time to actually think about the changes you want to make in your life, whether they are small or large.

Be realistic, don't set out some huge grand plan with an unachievable target in the timeframe you are allowing. You are much better off breaking this large resolution into smaller chunks, allowing yourself to deal with these manageable sized steps individually, possibly as you go through the year.

You also need to allow yourself to be flexible.

A New Year's resolution starts on one day, but a year is a long time and you need to allow yourself to change and adapt as you go through this time. You will learn different things as you move on in your resolution, so you should allow yourself to adapt and grow rather than focusing singularly on that one thing that you decided at the beginning of the year.

You also need to allow yourself to fall off the wagon a little. That's okay as long as you get back on. One chocolate bar doesn't mean that you need to give up on healthy eating altogether. One day off, lying on the couch in front of the TV does not mean that you need to give up your dream of running a marathon, and one patch of not writing the next chapter of your novel does not mean that you have to give up on it altogether.

You need to allow yourself to grow and change as the year goes on. You may find that your resolution needs to be adapted as you change. What you thought with your reasons and targets on January 1st may develop as you go through the year, and you find that far from taking a photo of something different every day to develop your photography skills, you actually want to focus on one subject and become an expert in that narrow field.

None of this matters.

All that matters is that you grow, and learn and develop and that on 1st January next year you are happier and more settled than you were on 1st January this year.

Why resolutions fail

Some of the statistics about resolutions, especially New Year's resolutions can be quite depressing.

Apparently the majority of resolutions are focused on self-improvement so they include things like exercising more, losing weight, giving up smoking or giving up alcohol or coffee.

According to Forbes in 2013, 40% of Americans made New Year's resolution but unfortunately only 8% of them achieve their target.

Reports show that about 75% of people keep their resolutions until 7th January, this drops to 71% by 14th January and to about 64% by 1st February.

Gym companies love January. So many people sign up for membership on 1st January and then are never seen again after 1st February.

So it seems clear that for many people the New Year's Resolution doesn't last that much longer than the New Year's Eve hangover.

There are lots of reasons why New Year's resolutions have such a high failure rate.

Some people just make too many resolutions at the same time, or they make them with no real intention of following through, or they make ones that are unrealistic and really have no chance of success.

Most of us live very busy lives, so adding a whole long list of new things to fit into your schedule is doomed from the start.

It's always better to start one resolution at a time and to make it as simple and straightforward as possible. If your overall life changing plan is large-scale, you can always add new resolutions as you succeed with the original one.

Start a new habit, develop it and let it become part of your life, then add the next one, until at the end of the year when you look back you are a different person.

You're also likely to be much more successful if you are specific in your New Year's resolution. Having a goal and a target rather than a vague wish is always going to be more successful.

You need willpower to be able to achieve your resolutions. Many people say they don't have any willpower, but that's not true. They always have the willpower to do something they actually want to do. The fact that they don't have the willpower to give up smoking or to lose weight or to get fitter is often because they haven't genuinely decided that they want to do that.

Saying that you want to do something is very, very different to actually believing that you want to do something.

One of the biggest reasons for failing in your New Year's resolution is to believe that you will fail even as you begin.

On some inner level, your inner voices are telling you that you have no chance of succeeding. You have to silence those inner voices right at the beginning. The fact is, that you can do anything you set your mind to, and believing that you can do it is the first step to success.

So you need to allow yourself to succeed.

One of the problems with a New Year's resolution, is that you often begin it when you are not mentally ready for it.

You might find yourself making the same resolution year in year out, only to give up on it after a few weeks each time.

If this is the case it's time to start thinking about why you are failing.

Are you picking something that you think you should do but you're not really interested in doing? Are you surrounded by pressure to give up alcohol but find that you really enjoy a glass of wine and simply don't have the willpower to give it up. After all what's wrong with a glass of wine?

You have to actually want and feel the need to change your habits rather than simply being pushed by pressure from friends, fashion or reading the latest list in a magazine or newspaper.

If you do set and fail the same resolution every year, take time to think seriously about what you are doing. This can be quite a difficult process because it means that you have to be honest with yourself and actually look into your deeper feelings and emotions, but a resolution has to mean something to you before it is ever going to succeed.

So, the giving up alcohol.

If you look seriously at yourself, how much alcohol do you consume? If it's a glass or two of wine once or twice a week, do you really feel the need to give it up just to follow the fashion? However if it's a bottle of wine every evening, then you do need to think seriously about it and probably need a little help in working towards reducing your dependency on alcohol and improving your health. If that's the case, then giving up alcohol would be a very worthwhile New Year's resolution and one that you should treat seriously.

Giving up alcohol is just an example. There can be many resolutions which we set and fail year after year, but which deep down we realise they are important for our health and happiness, and setting a resolution is a very good way of giving you the impetus to follow through and to strengthen your willpower.

Do not see your resolution as one big package that has to be dealt with and successfully finished on day one.

If you look at it that way then the first slip - and there will be slips - will see you give up altogether and become just another one of those statistics on failure. But if you see it as the start of the new journey, and you take it one step at a time, in small chunks, growing as you go through the year, then you have much better chance of succeeding, and success is what this book is about.

Types of New Year's resolution.

A New Year's resolution can be about anything you want to be. It is a plan to change your life for the better, so of course it is a very personal journey and it can be about anything that you feel you need to do to improve your life.

Having said that there are of course some common New Year's resolutions that cover many different changes you might need to make in life and this list should give you something to think about as you're planning your New Year's resolution.

Getting healthy.

This can cover all sorts of areas such as eating healthier food, losing weight, getting fitter and exercising more often, giving up alcohol, giving up smoking or giving up biting your nails. It can be any habit that you feel you need to break in order to become healthier, or anything you think you need to change in your life to reach the same target.

Getting mentally healthy.

Mental well-being is very important to a happier life and health in general so you may decide that your resolution is to be more positive, to smile more, to laugh more often and to open your eyes and see what life can offer you so that you can just enjoy life rather than looking for the negative.

Financial fitness.

This can be a major life changing plan and if followed through can come completely transform your life. You may want to get out of debt or save money or even start investing money and planning for the future.

Career planning.

Many people want to make changes in their career and they use New Year's resolutions to give them that spurt. As long as you make a good plan you can aim to do better at work, go for a promotion, change jobs or even careers, you might even want to start your own business.

Pursuing education.

You might resolve to improve your grades, or to continue education. You could take on training either to improve your career, to widen your life skills or for relaxation.

Giving back.

You might decide that it is time to start volunteering, to give something back to your community, indeed to become part of your community.

Improving your home.

This is an increasingly popular area for New Year's resolutions. Some people want to de-clutter, spring cleaning has moved forward a few months. Some people want to redecorate, renovate or relocate altogether.

Resolutions can be about any area of your life. There are many things that you know you want to make changes in, and if you're serious about it, the New Year with its new opportunities and its fresh new start, can be an ideal time to start making these changes. You might want to spend more time with your family or indeed to settle down and start a new family.

You might decide that this is the year you should start to travel and to see some more of the world.

You might feel that you need to embrace spirituality in your life, and a New Year's resolution can give you that push to really do something about it rather than continually putting it off.

As you've read through this list, see if any of the ideas have struck a chord with you personally. I've put some more ideas at the end of this book.

Before you go any further sit down with pen and paper, or with a fresh page on your computer screen and put down some ideas for your own life and the changes or improvements you would like to make.

Are there things you would like to give up?

Are there things that you would like to start?

Are there plans and dreams that you have had for a long time but have never done anything about?

Think seriously, think deeply. Don't get caught up in the whole New Year's Eve and New Year's Day, magazine reading, party mode. Think calmly about what you would truly like to have done by the end of the year and then plan your path to get there.

Winning the resolution battle

Josie Baxter

Setting a goal

Now that we know what resolutions are and why we set them, the next stage is to make sure that you can succeed.

One of the main problems with traditional resolutions is that they are more of a wish list than a plan.

As I said earlier a goal without a plan is just wish.

If you want to have success in your resolutions, then you need goals.

If you have traditionally been the person who sets New Year's resolutions every year, they probably go along the lines of I want to lose weight, I hope I'll be fitter this year, I wish I could be more successful.

The problem with this is that none of them really mean anything. If you really want to lose weight, get fitter or be more successful you need to set an active goal that you can work towards every day.

For instance, if you have picked one of the really popular resolutions I want to lose weight, instead of being very general about it, set an actual goal. I will lose 10lbs in 10 weeks.

This is an example of a good goal. It has a specific target in a specific timeframe. The fact that it is clear, you can measure it and you can judge whether you've been successful or not, is what makes it a good goal and you are much more likely to succeed once you set a good goal.

Albert Einstein said, 'if you want to live a happy life, tie it to a goal, not to people or things.'

When you are deciding on your goal, make sure that it will work for you.

A successful goal should be SMART.
- Specific
- Measurable
- Attainable
- Relevant
- Time based

Picking the right goals and making sure that they are achievable will make the difference between achieving what you set out to do when setting your New Year's resolution, or being one of those statistics on failure.

Setting a **specific** goal means that you avoid being vague which is often a problem with resolutions. It means that you clearly focus on what your goal is and what steps you will take to meet these goals.

Measuring your progress allows you to see how things are working for you and to enjoy the progress you are making.

Attainable goals will allow you to be successful. It's all very well reaching for the stars, but it does help if the star that you have targeted is actually within reach with a bit of effort.

Relevant goals will actually mean something to you. Following fashion and peer pressure is all very well, but if a goal doesn't actually mean something to you, you will have no real interest in achieving it and - surprise, surprise - you will be very unlikely to achieve it.

Setting a **time scale** makes your goal real. Deadlines are very useful, they are a target, a line in the sand, a reason to get to a specific point in a specific timeframe. It makes your goal real rather than just one of those wishes.

Making your resolution a goal.

But how do you make your resolution into a goal?
Write it down.

The best way to make something real is to put it on paper. Even in this modern day where everything is on computers and smartphones and tablets, there is still something very real about a piece of paper.

Personally, I love writing with a fountain pen, even the first draft of this book is being written with a fountain pen in a notepad, I just think more clearly that way. I'm quite happy to then put it onto the computer and edit from the screen, but for some reason pen on paper is more real. And it's not only me that finds that.

Even in our modern age there is something much more real about actually committing something to paper. You might be able to tear out the page from the notepad, screw it up and throw it in the bin, but that's not quite the same as just hitting delete.

So sit down with pen and paper (it doesn't have to be a fountain pen – not really!) and write out a list of things that you want to consider as your resolutions.

Once you have this in front of you, it is easier to see patterns, do they all have something in common?

Are they all really small parts of one big resolution?

If they are, you could organise them as steps to your greater goal.

You need to be focused when you set a New Year's resolution if you want to have a good chance of success.

There is no point in writing out a bucket list of resolutions. If there are too many you have no chance of succeeding in any of them, you will simply skip from one to the other without any real focus and without any real chance of success.

So once you have your list, look at it clearly and decide what you actually want to deal with in the coming year.

Pick the thing that is most important to you, after all you can always set aside the other ideas for next year.

So choose something that you really, genuinely want to change about your life. It is much easier to make something a goal that you can work towards if you discover that it's something you really want to do.

Identifying this one thing can be a little difficult and you do have to genuinely, seriously and deeply think about it. You are not going to find the one thing in life that you want to tackle and that you want to change, by just reading through a magazine list of the standard, sometimes trite and overused resolution ideas.

So take this stage seriously this time, think about what changes you want in your life, what changes will actually matter to you.

Where would you like to see yourself in a years' time?

What changes in your life are worth working at, are worth giving things up for, are worth putting the effort into?

A genuine resolution should aim to make your life better.

Your idea of better is personal and only you can decide on what that is. Do you want to be fitter? Do you want to be happier? Do you want to make the move you've always planned but never seem to do? Do you want to take that next step in your career?

What is it that matters to you?

What do you want your future to be?

Once you have decided on this, you will find it so much easier to focus on your goal, because it will be important to you.

It doesn't matter if it is a huge target or really small, what matters is that it will make a change in your life that you really want.

How to set a successful goal.

So you need to create a goal that means something to you.

If it means something to you it means that you will be prepared to put your energy into it. It also means that you can set a plan of action for yourself on how you are going to achieve your goal.

You might want to join a group, you might want to purchase some fitness equipment, you might want to de-clutter and rid yourself of anything that might tempt you to give in.

This preparation is always a good first stage. It's far harder to give up smoking if you leave all the lighters and ashtrays lying around, in the same way as it is far harder to stick to a diet if your cupboard is full of crisps and biscuits. That is one of the things that can make the lose weight resolution really difficult. After all you're picking a time of year where you have filled the house with unhealthy food.

So the first step is to prepare the ground. Don't leave temptation lying around, don't put obstacles in your way and don't allow other people to ridicule your goal.

Once you have prepared your ground and your mindset you are ready to move onto the next step.

Set out a specific goal and timetable.

It always helps when a goal is specific, and the clearer it is, the more likely you are to succeed.

After all, if you don't have a target how do you know when you have hit it?

I always set a deadline when I'm writing a book, otherwise the process just goes on forever!

A specific goal can be clearly defined.

For instance, I will be able to run 2 miles by 1st February rather than, I want to be able to run 2 miles.

If you don't set yourself a time target, a deadline, you have nothing to aim for and no way to measure your success, which makes it much easier to put off reaching your goal.

If your resolution is financial you also have to make sure that you set achievable steps and targets.

You might decide you want to be a millionaire, but if your plan simply relies on winning the lottery it's a wish not a goal.

If you genuinely want to work towards being a millionaire, you have to look seriously at where you are at the moment and work out how you can increase your income from where you are to where you want to be. This might mean retraining, setting up a business that you can run while still working, working your way up through the property ladder or learning how to invest (although you should only do this with money you can afford to lose).

Success relies on setting successful goals. And this very often means breaking your large goal into smaller more achievable goals. After all it might take you a few years to become a millionaire or to be able to win a triathlon.

When you divide a larger goal into smaller, achievable chunks it immediately becomes more manageable and it means that you won't be overwhelmed by the magnitude of the task in front of you. As they say, the longest journey begins with a single step.

It can also be helpful to share your goals with someone close to you and important to you.

Choose someone who will support and help you along the way, you certainly don't want to share your goals with someone who will ridicule you. But somebody who will support you, will help you and you will feel more accountable if you know that someone else will be aware that you are giving up.

Goal setting tips

- Goals should be personally meaningful.
- You should have an action plan.
- Plan your steps.
- Break large goals into smaller chunks.
- Believe in your ability to succeed.
- Allow yourself to be flexible.
- Make your goals specific not vague.
- Set target dates for all the steps.
- Set realistic goals.
- But have the confidence to dream big.
- Be honest about what is holding you back.
- Visualise your success.
- Write your goals down.
- Allow yourself rewards for reaching your targets.
- Work on your goal every day.

Creating life goals.

As you can see, a truly successful New Year's resolution is actually far more important and far deeper than we tend to think.

If you prefer, you can spend the rest of your life setting and failing with meaningless resolutions that you have no genuine interest in and no real thought of succeeding.

That might be fun, a bit of a game at the New Year's Eve party, but it's pointless and it won't get you anywhere. It is just a game.

If you want genuine resolutions that will genuinely change your life, and if you're reading this book you probably do, then they deserve deeper thought.

One of the main benefits about thinking deeply about the New Year's resolution, is that it helps you think about what you want from life. Many experts suggest that you should set individual goals for different areas of your life. This can help make you more rounded as a person, more successful, happier and more satisfied with life in general.

The main areas that are suggested are:
- Family and home life goals.
- Physical and health goals.
- Financial and career goals.

- Social and cultural goals.
- Mental and educational goals.
- Spiritual and ethical goals.

Personally, I feel that having strong spiritual and ethical goals are a good framework for any other goals in your life, as they can be your strength and provide you with your guiding principles.

Spending some time thinking about these lifetime goals is a very good way of actually creating a plan for your life. Many people simply drift through life without having any focus or plan about where they want to be.

Although this isn't necessarily bad, it means that some people are constantly able to take opportunities when they arise, to change direction as they feel the need and to live a full, exciting and challenging life. But unfortunately for most people, it means getting to a point in life, looking back and being disappointed.

Being disappointed that they didn't get the home they really wanted.

Being disappointed that their career didn't go anywhere.

Being disappointed that they don't have a comfortable retirement plan, that they didn't spend more time with their family, that they spent too much time working and not enough time relaxing and enjoying life.

It isn't always a lack of money or opportunity that leads to disappointment.

Some people reach a stage in their life where they are very comfortably off, but they have no one to share it with.

Knowing where you want to go in life gives you a much better chance of getting there. And that's where life goals can be so valuable.

Maybe your first New Year's resolution should be to create a plan for your life goals.

A goal is always more real when it is detailed. And as I've already said, I always find it much more real if I write it down, pen on paper.

Life goals are necessarily big.

Your physical and health goals for life are more than losing a few pounds or being able to run 2 miles.

So take one life area at a time and really think about what you want to achieve in life for that area.

For instance, if you are thinking about your family and home life goals you might want to be able to buy a larger house.

Think about what this house will look like. Where will it be? What are the main features you want, swimming pool, a garage, a games room, a large garden? What facilities do you want close to your home? The good school, local shops, a good transport network, easy access to an outdoor life?

Write all of this down, being as detailed as you can. Can you smell the fresh flowers? Can you see the furniture? Can you see the views?

This is your goal.

When you spend this long thinking about something, you work out what it is you really want rather than the grand scheme on TV or a fancy magazine layout. Spending time thinking about what you actually want helps you create a realistic goal in life and then you can set about working out how to achieve that.

After all I live in the north-east of England the ancient Kingdom of Northumbria, an area full of amazing, genuine castles, many of them with a history of almost a thousand years.

I love castles – the history, the romance, the style - but I'm also aware that it wouldn't be at all practical for me to dream about buying a castle (although I know someone who did)!

It would be far too big, far too costly to heat (this is the north-east of England) and just totally unrealistic, but that doesn't mean I wouldn't have a painting of a castle on the wall of my library in my more modest house!

So work through the different areas of your life and decide what to your goals are, what will create a successful, fulfilled and happy life for you.

We are all worth a happy life.

There is no reason that we cannot take the opportunities we have and create what we want out of them. You just need a plan and the ability to follow that plan through.

When you are making these life goals, remember that they are your life goals. Not everyone really wants to live the big dream, and there's no reason you should feel pressurised into following somebody else's dream or the marketing man's idea of success. When you take the time to really think about what you want from life you might decide that it isn't the big career, the big house, big car and expensive holidays. Even if you do have that lifestyle at the moment, it might not be making you happy and you might discover that what you really want is to be self-sufficient and live the simple life in the country.

Be honest with yourself in this process.

It's not about what your parents think you should have, it is not what your friends think you should have, it is not even what your partner thinks you should have. It's what you know will ultimately make you happier.

Once you have this plan for your life goals you will be able to decide which of them you should tackle first and how you can create meaningful, achievable and genuine resolutions for your New Year.

After all, one of the saddest phrases is *I wish I had done that.*

Tracking your success.

Writing out your goals is the first step towards success, but you need to know that you are actually getting somewhere.

This means that you always need to record and track your success.

As I said earlier, one of the best ways of being able to succeed with your resolutions is to break down a large task into small manageable chunks.

When you have written down your grand plan and your overall goal, it you should also write down the stages towards completing this goal.

You can now turn these stages into a system for keeping track of where you are on your path.

For instance, if your resolution is to lose weight or to embrace healthy eating, you could keep a food journal.

This can seem quite daunting at first, to write down everything that you eat every day whether that is a full meal or a biscuit, but the thing, is once you see it in black and white it becomes more real and it is far easier to see exactly what you're doing, where you could be making mistakes and where you are being successful.

Once you can see exactly what you are doing you can adapt your plan to suit your lifestyle, for instance you may snack a lot more at weekends, or drink more wine than you thought on Friday night. If you can see that this is part of your routine, you can then decide whether to work at cutting it out, or whether to adjust your overall plan to allow for a treat that is important to you.

At the other extreme, by writing everything down, you may discover you're actually not eating enough calories to keep you healthy and fit.

We always think that we know what we are doing, but when you make a record of it, it's quite often the fact that what you think you are doing is not what you're really doing at all.

You can track anything that you have set as a New Year's resolution.

If health and fitness is your goal, there are now many fitness trackers that help keep you on the right lines and let you know the steps you've taken how many flights of stairs you have used and your overall distance each day.

You can also track your success by setting up a specific plan.

For instance, your goal may be financially based, either to get out of debt, save money in general, or to save for a specific target such as a holiday, a wedding or a new home.

This is a very worthy idea in general, and you will start with the best of intentions on 1st January, but will you have saved anything by 1st February?

What is your plan to achieve this target?

Setting up a system and then tracking that system is a much surer way to be successful than just leaving it to chance.

You could think that you will spend less money as the month goes on, saving by cutting out that latte, trip to the cinema or night out. Then your plan is to take the money you haven't spent and is therefore is left in your account and transfer to a savings account.

How much do you think will be left at the end of January?

If you're like most other people, the answer will be very little. Money just has this habit of evaporating!

However, if you set up a savings account and treat your saving as you would treat any other bill - something that has to be paid - you will be much more successful.

Set up a regular payment from your main account into the savings account and keep that separate account specifically for the money towards your goal.

This means that you can track your success, you can see the money filtering in every month and you will hardly even notice that has gone. Over time you may feel that you can increase the amount, it can be quite addictive to watch your savings grow.

As with any resolution, don't be too unrealistic when you set your original amount. Suddenly deciding that 50% of your income can be saved is probably unmanageable, which means that you will fail and you will lose confidence altogether. However setting 5% or 10% aside can be surprisingly manageable, and you can always increase it over time. You may even decide to take on a part-time job or find some other way to increase your income and therefore the amount you can save.

Keeping track of what you are doing can be adjusted to suit any resolution or goal in life and it is a very important tool in your success kit.

Being able to track the individual steps on your road to success makes a resolution much more real and much more achievable, and is one of the important ways to ensure that this time your New Year's resolution will be life changing instead of just another failure

Create new habits.

Any resolution is really a matter of creating new habits.

If your goal is very large, then breaking it down into manageable chunks makes it much easier to achieve, and this really means that you are creating lots of small habits, working you towards your overall goal.

Trying to change your entire life in one go is just too large a task to have any chance of succeeding.

It seems like a wonderful target when you first think of it, but you're only human, and as humans we just cannot change everything at once. It is overwhelming and you are simply setting yourself up for failure and disappointment.

But creating smaller new habits can be a great way of achieving your goal.

After all if you look at a mountain it can seem insurmountable and certainly unclimbable, but even a mountain can be broken down one little pebble at a time, even if it will be a very long time.

So if your New Year's resolution is to get fitter, don't start by joining the gym and spending two hours of circuit training every day, that's probably a good way to make you give up altogether. But if you create a new habit of

Resolve to succeed

parking at the opposite end of the car park and walking the rest of the way, that will quickly become a habit. Then you can start to use the stairs instead of the lift, maybe creating the habit for one floor at a time. Then you can decide that you are going to walk to the local store for bottled milk or newspaper every day instead of just getting them in the supermarket shop. Before you know where you are you will be doing a lot more exercise than you ever thought possible and you can add to these new habits all the time even by joining that gym.

We all think that we slip into bad habits, but good habits are just as easy to form.

Getting into the habit of picking up a banana as a snack instead of a doughnut.

Getting into the habit of drinking water instead of a fizzy drink, or getting into the habit of putting the loose change in a savings jar instead of buying a coffee with it.

There's a lot of information about breaking old habits and forming new habits and how long it should take. If you look on the Internet you will find information that says it is anywhere from 21 days to a year.

The thing is that none of this advice allows for the fact that creating a new habit to eat a piece of fruit every day, is not in the same league as breaking a habit that is a central part of your life such as smoking, drinking or spending every evening sitting in front of the TV.

Be kind to yourself. If you expect to have formed a new habit that has become unshakeable in 21 days, when you get today 22 and find that you are still having to put some effort into it, you will feel as if you have failed.

So allow time.

In general, two months is a much more realistic timeframe than 21 days. You need to allow your subconscious to adapt and become used to this new habit. If you miss eating your apple on one day it is not a disaster, just make sure you eat it the next day.

If you've decided to give up cakes but then find yourself at a birthday celebration, don't beat yourself up about it, you can avoid the cakes again the next day.

If you take an all or nothing approach to your New Year's resolution and to creating your new habits, then when you slip up - and you will - you're much more likely to give up altogether instead of just starting fresh again the next day.

It can help if you give yourself some encouragement in creating your new habits. You could say them out loud to yourself, this can help reinforce them in your mind. You can also write a note to yourself, maybe a Post-it note that you then stick on your bathroom mirror or your computer monitor.

Reminding yourself of your goals and reinforcing your personal resolutions in your mind can help you to keep them more real and relevant, and this can help you stick with your plan rather than being another statistic who had given up by February.

Don't get distracted.

It's so easy to get distracted.

There are so many things that can lead you off track, that can take your attention. Modern life is full of things that can divert you from your plan or make you lose your focus, and of course this is why we give up most of our plans. We don't actively give them up, we just become distracted and forget about them or just keep putting it off until tomorrow.

But if you want to succeed, if you want to reach your goals, if you want your resolutions to actually mean something, then you have to stay focused.

Let's face it it's far easier to sit on the sofa with another pack of crisps, rather than go out for that two-mile run you promised yourself, we are talking New Year's resolutions, so for an awful lot of us that means cold, wet, dark January evenings, and if your New Year's resolution is to get fitter and more active you probably couldn't have picked a worse time of the year to start!

But if you have decided to start as a New Year's resolution, then you need a plan to help you overcome the cold, wet, dark weather that you will be dealing with.

The same is true if your resolution is to lose weight or eat more healthy food. This is a very difficult time of year to do it. Winter is for comfort food not salads.

You could say the same thing for a number of different resolutions, for instance saving money or paying off debts. January can be one of the most difficult months financially as you pay off all the costs of Christmas.

So it's important to be aware of these potential distractions and pitfalls as you plan for your resolution.

Don't make unrealistic demands on yourself, you are not going to cycle to work instead of driving the car in the middle of a snowstorm. So do your research and think about it as you prepare for a New Year and new you.

If you plan for it, you can avoid some of the distractions. For instance, you can make sure you've plenty of recipes and ingredients for filling, warming foods that are still healthy and full of goodness. You can make your plan for saving but also plan to implement it from February not January 1st.

There are also some types of distraction you can avoid.

If you don't go into the coffee shop, you won't be tempted to buy a muffin with your take-out coffee, so buy yourself a travel mug and take your morning coffee from home.

If you don't go to the wine and beer aisle in the supermarket, you will not be tempted by the offer on Shiraz, which means that you won't be tempted to buy a bottle, take it home and drink it. The same goes for avoiding the aisle with chocolates in it.

Everybody has different weaknesses and different points of temptation, and you know what your own are. So don't make life more difficult than it needs to be. It's far easier to avoid the temptation if it isn't in front of you.

One of the other things that can distract you from your goals, is a tendency towards perfectionism.

Many people have the idea that if they cannot get it right straightaway, if they cannot be perfect, then they may as well give up altogether.

Nobody is perfect.

Certainly nobody is good at everything, and nobody becomes an expert overnight. Experts have spent years practising and they continue to practice, and they are willing to practice to be as good as they can possibly be.

So why should you expect yourself to get things right straightaway?

But the problem for many people, is that this desire to get it right straightaway, and of course the failure to do that, is one of the main reasons that they fail year after year in their resolutions.

I can't stick to it, I can't get it right, I'm not succeeding, I may as well give up altogether. That is the kind of mental reasoning that leads to failure.

But the fact is, that it's part of human nature to trip. It's natural to give into a craving or miss an exercise class. The difference between failure and success is to pick up where you left off and carry on with your journey to reaching your goal. Giving into a craving is fine as long as you accept it and start again the next day. Missing an exercise class is okay as long as that doesn't mean you give up on the class altogether.

So don't see the occasional trip in your journey as a terminal crash. See where you've gone wrong, try to decide what it was that caused you to go wrong and continue on your path.

Obstacles are there to be overcome, they're all part of the journey.

You should also be willing to accept help or support from others. There's no point trying to reinvent the wheel. Someone else has probably found a technique or method that could help you in sticking to your resolution, so you should be prepared to be open-minded and to accept new ideas and new methods. If you find that you are having trouble with your resolution, look around, do some research, ask your friends or be prepared to listen to someone else. You might find advice that will help you in your path towards your goal.

Staying positive is another very important part of succeeding in anything.

Believing that you can succeed keeps you open and positive and focused on your goal, rather than allowing negative thoughts to push you off the path altogether.

If you are having trouble with staying positive, try using some positive affirmations. After all we are what our brain tells us we are. If you have been told for years that you will never be a success, that you will never be slim, that you will never be fit, that you will never have money - it's natural that subconsciously you will believe this.

But this is your life, your plan, your goals, your future. It isn't up to anybody else to say what you can do or what you can be, and if you feel you need some help in retraining your brain to believe this, then positive affirmations can really help.

In any type of learning, repetition helps make pathways in the brain so that something becomes subconscious as we learn how to do it.

The same is true of beliefs.

So if somebody has told you for many years that you are a failure you will believe that. Now is the time to start telling yourself every day that you can succeed, that you are good enough.

Speak the words out loud, visualise and verbalise what your goal is and each time you say that positive message to yourself, your brain will create new pathways and you will get closer and closer to success.

This path of progress is a very important part of reaching your goals and keeping to your resolutions. Small steps are valuable, note and appreciate them, every one of those small steps gets you nearer to your goal and makes your success more achievable.

Declare your intentions.

As we've seen, the statistics are not good for succeeding with your resolutions, most people simply give up.

Giving up on your goals is never good, but if you're the only one who knows you have failed, then at least it's not embarrassing. You don't have to face others and tell them you've given up.

And that is why it is very useful to declare your intentions to others when you have a serious, life changing goal in mind. The fact that other people will be watching makes it much more likely that you will stick to the plan.

If you tell yourself that you're going to run 12 marathons in 12 days to raise money for your favourite charity, and you find that after six months you haven't even run a half marathon, you've let yourself down. You might even have let your charity down, but only in your own mind, after all you never told them you were going to raise money for them.

But imagine doing that if you've told all your friends, you've told the charity, you've put it on Facebook you've even told the local newspaper. You would move heaven and earth to do those 12 marathons. You would train as

Resolve to succeed

hard as you could, you would plan, you would set out timetables, you would raise funds and chase sponsorship. You would do everything in your power to succeed because the cost of failing would be more than you are prepared to face.

Now most of us don't have goals to run 12 marathons in 12 days. But we do have goals that are important to us, that can change our lives, goals that are worth working towards.

So if you feel that this extra push of expectation from other people will help you and strengthen your willpower then think of ways to declare your intentions to others that will suit your lifestyle.

- You could write a note to friends and family.
- you could put it on Facebook or Twitter.
- You could make a pledge to your partner.
- You could start a blog.
- You could email your friends.
- You could spell it out on your fridge.

There are lots of ways to declare your intentions to other people, and the way that you choose and the people you choose to tell will depend on your lifestyle.

But don't do this at the New Year's Eve party!

You really need to have thought this through, because once you declare your intentions to others you will find that you have to follow through.

Letting yourself down in private is totally different to letting yourself down in front of all your friends.

Making the decision to declare your intentions and become personally accountable can be quite a big change in your life.

It is absolutely vital in this process that you are true to yourself, you are putting your goals and your resolutions out there in public and you will have to live with them.

This means that you will have to accept that you are responsible for the way you live, the way you think and how you deal with certain situations. You will have to accept responsibility for failures as well as your successes, life does not go smoothly at all times.

It's easy to accept responsibility for your successes and the good things that happen in life, but many people are unable to accept responsibility when things go wrong. They always look for someone else to blame, it is always somebody else's fault. If you want to succeed in reaching your goals, then you will have to learn to accept responsibility for when things go wrong as well as when things go right. You cannot change what is wrong if you don't accept responsibility in the first place.

You also have to be able to stop living in the past.

So many people do live in the past. In fact, they find it almost impossible to let go and move on. But you have to accept that what has happened is over and done with. No one has a time machine, no one can go back and change things, all you can do is learn from the past to improve the future.

Wasting time on what if's and should have's, will only hold you back and stop you reaching that success that is waiting for you.

Being accountable.

Being personally accountable can be a powerful tool in life. Once you take responsibility for your own life instead of allowing others to control you and your life, you are on the path to self-empowerment.

This can be the case in any area of your life. There is a difference between fitting in and just being a follower.

Following the rules of society or your chosen career, fitting in with your families and friends are important, not everyone can be a maverick. But when you allow others to pull your strings you are giving up control and the ability to reach your own goals.

Another huge mistake, is to fall into the habit of always blaming something or someone else for what happens to you. If you do this then you have given away your responsibility for your own life and you can hardly expect to reach your goals when you don't control your own life.

So if you want to learn how to make things happen in your life and how to achieve your goals and be successful in your resolutions, you have to allow yourself to become self-empowered.

This means accepting the risks of taking positive action.

Instead of waiting for opportunities and people to come to you, you have to go out and chase down your dreams.

Unless you learn this particular skill, you will never control your own life. You will always be waiting for things to happen to you rather than making things happen for your future.

This can be a little scary, especially if you've been the type of person who always just trundles along accepting what life throws at them. Sometimes life throws some goodies, you may be comfortable, settled, not unhappy. But if you are serious about changing your life, setting goals and following your resolutions, then you are looking for something more than comfortable, better than settled and much more than not unhappy. You want to be successful, fulfilled, excited and overjoyed at your success.

So you have to set expectations of yourself. You need to know what you expect from your goal, after all if you don't know what you are looking for how will you know when you find it?

Making a successful resolution is an indication that you want to make changes in your life, very often big changes and this means taking control, being able to accept your mistakes when something goes wrong.

If you are in the habit of always blaming someone something else when things don't go according to plan, you are never going to be able to learn from your mistakes. You have to be able to be honest with yourself because brutal honesty is one of the main requirements of being able to change your life, keep your resolutions, achieve your goals.

So when you look at your goal or plan your New Year's resolution, you also need to take a serious look as to why you have not succeeded in this before.

And as I say - be honest - don't make excuses, don't skirt around the issue.

There is no point in cheating or lying, you would only be cheating and lying to yourself. You are the only one who can hold yourself accountable for your actions.

If you truly want to lose weight or to have a healthier diet, you have to be strong enough to give up the crisps and biscuits or whatever else is your thing. There's no point in telling yourself you didn't have time to get a proper meal, you were exhausted and needed a sugar fix, everybody else was eating crisps or you were too busy running around after the kids and only had time for a biscuit.

Who are you giving the excuses to? You're only cheating on yourself. You are the one who wants to lose weight and get healthier, so you are the one who has to take responsibility for it and telling yourself that a biscuit with a cup of coffee doesn't count is just a lie and you know with this. So if you want to succeed in your resolutions you have to decide to be honest with yourself and to accept responsibility for your actions.

As you learn to accept responsibility and to be accountable for your actions it will begin to have effects in all sorts of areas of your life not just in your ability to succeed in your resolution.

Being accountable and responsible means that other people will respect you more, which means that you are more likely to receive a promotion at work, to be taken more seriously by your friends and family. This in turn will have a positive effect on you as you become more confident, begin to believe in yourself or and to believe that you can be successful.

Have an accountability partner.

Many people find it much easier to stick to a goal if they work with someone or in a group.

A very good example of this is when you join a weight loss program. The fact that you are going to a meeting once a week and have to stand up and tell others what you have done and whether you have lost weight or not is a great motivator.

Likewise having a gym buddy means that you're much more likely to go to the gym or the exercise class, partly because you don't want to let someone else down and partly because you don't want to be seen as a quitter.

We are social animals and we like belonging to groups. We also find the social influence and peer pressure of other people very powerful and that can make all the difference to your resolution lasting past the end of January. Letting yourself down is one thing, letting other people down is often much more difficult. So if that is what motivates you, then find an accountability partner.

You should put some thought into this.

You need to find somebody that you are comfortable with, someone you can share your fears with, without feeling embarrassed or ashamed. In many cases, it's important that you can be honest with each other.

So when you're looking for a partner, you need to understand why you are doing that and what you expect to receive from a partner. Some people work best with gentle encouragement, whereas others find that a sergeant major type will push them onwards to success.

A good accountability partner is not necessarily someone who is close to you. Your best friend or your partner may not feel able to tell you where you are failing or losing focus, and even if they do you might not be willing to listen.

So think about what you are looking for, different goals and resolutions were required different types of accountability partners.

If your resolution is to get fitter or lose weight you might find it best to join a club or a group where others have the same goal.

If your target is business or career related, you might find an accountability partner in one of your professional groups or forums.

Depending on what your goal resolution is, you may even be able to find an accountability partner online in one of the chat rooms or forums that are particularly related to your goal, although you should always take care when making any contacts online.

As a general guide, working with an accountability partner is always best if you can do it in person, setting regular meetings so that you can map your progress.

When you are setting your meetings it's best to have an agenda for it so that you can spend time discussing any obstacles or struggles that you may be having, and come up with a plan to find a solution. If you don't have this agenda in mind it's too easy to simply chat and achieve nothing.

A good accountability partner will help you understand your task in reaching your goal, help you accept the steps you have to take and help you set a deadline.

A deadline is always very important.

You will also have to be prepared to accept responsibility if you do not meet your deadline and you must be able to explain why you haven't.

Obviously there will be times when life just gets in the way and other things have to take priority, but it's important not to get into a habit of finding excuses for missing a deadline. If you are constantly failing to achieve what you set out to do you, might need to find a different course of action or a different way of reaching your goal.

Whenever you take on a new task, you learn things on the journey, and you may well learn that your initial goal is not exactly right. If that is the case there is nothing wrong with adapting your plan, as long as you accept that things have changed and you need to change with them. This is the difference between succeeding with your resolution and just giving up altogether.

Willpower is fine, obstinacy can cause problems.

Benefits of accountability.

There are many benefits to having an accountability plan. Once it's in place you will find that you worry less because you are finally taking action and making progress towards your goal. You have a plan to carry through your resolution.

You will also find that your mind is much more focused, you are able to concentrate on what is important to you rather than being distracted all the time.

Once your goal becomes real, it is worth pursuing, it is worth dedicating time and energy to. It is an investment worth making because you have a target in mind and you're going to improve your life.

You'll probably find that you are much more alert and attentive in general because your mind is focused rather than drifting. You finally have a goal in your life, you are working towards something you may have wanted for years, but this time you actually have a plan on how to get to it.

If you have an accountability partner, you are also learning how to rely on others, how to open your mind to different opinions and different ideas rather than just being stuck in your own personal rut.

I'm not suggesting that this is going to be all easy, in fact it can be quite hard.

You have to be prepared to accept advice from someone else if you have an accountability partner.

You have to be prepared to be uncomfortable with their opinion sometimes, you may not want to hear the truth all the time. But it's a pain barrier that is worth pushing through.

Once you learn to become personally accountable, you will feel much more in control of your life and much happier.

Stress is very often caused by being out of control, so once you take control, stress, tension, dissatisfaction and general unhappiness can become part of your past.

Being practical – sticking to your goals

Josie Baxter

Create an action plan

So now you know what you should do, what is best way of going about it?

There are lots of techniques to help you turn that wish into reality, to help your New Year's resolution succeed instead of just being another failure.

If you follow the steps you are on the right path to making genuine, valuable changes in your life.

As we've seen earlier, the best way of succeeding in a resolution or reaching a goal is to break it down into manageable chunks.

When you have written out your list of steps, you should create a weekly or daily To Do List.

You might find it easiest if you can fit this into your daily routine, putting your actionable steps for your goal into your daily schedule along with getting the kids to school, doctor's appointments, going to work and doing the shopping.

Obviously, everybody's life is different and your personal schedule will depend on how many commitments you have. But putting the steps to reach your goal into your schedule in the same way as you would put work items and household or family commitments, makes them more real, more a part of your normal routine and much more likely to actually get done.

It makes the steps in your goal real, not something you would like to do if only you have time.

Having it written down means that you can see that you are achieving the steps you want. Being able to cross items off your list gives you a great sense of satisfaction, it means that you have accomplished something, that you are actually getting somewhere.

You can use this system for any type of goal or resolution, because no matter what you want to achieve there will be steps along the way, and it is by taking these small steps that you will be successful.

The key to motivation is to have a detailed list of steps, something that you can achieve each day and something that you can see that you have achieved.

Once you write something down, created a list or are using a spreadsheet, you have started to make your goal real rather than a dream, because a goal only becomes real once you have a plan on how you will achieve it.

Create deadlines.

Deadlines are wonderful things. People might worry about them but a deadline is a reason to complete whatever you are working on, otherwise they could just go on for eternity.

So whether you have a deadline for a book, for instance this one really needs to be out before New Year! Or a deadline of losing weight for a holiday, getting fit enough to run a marathon in six months' time, or having cleared your debts by the end of the year. A deadline is a target, and a target means you have something definite to aim at.

If your main deadline is longer term, then set yourself a collection of mini deadlines to get there, otherwise it is too easy to leave the whole thing to the last minute and you can't train for a marathon in the last two weeks. So schedule mini deadlines, put them on your to-do list and tick them off as you reach each one.

Announce your goals.

Having the confidence to let the world know that you have set a new goal or made a resolution can be a wonderful way of making sure that you will work towards success.

After all you don't want to let yourself down in front of all those people.

Think seriously before you do this, because - you don't want to let yourself down in front of all those people!

You must be absolutely sure that you are serious in your intention before taking this step. This means that it is not something to blog about, Facebook about or Twitter about under the influence of too much alcohol at the New Year's Eve party. You do not want to wake up on New Year's Day with a hangover, to discover that you've announced to the world that you are going to sell all your possessions and live in a tent to raise money for charity. If that is genuinely what you want to do it is a very noble idea, but it's very extreme and you're probably going to regret it.

Serious resolutions and life goals are by their very nature serious. But if you have put the thought into it and decided that this is what you want to do, telling the world is a very good way of helping you to stay on track.

An accountability partner.

Most people find doing anything alone is difficult. If you have no one else who will know you given up it's far easier to give up. Letting yourself down is so much easier than letting someone else down. And that's the very reason that working with an accountability partner can be such a wonderful idea. It helps you stay on track and stay motivated. Having to explain to someone else why you didn't turn up at the gym is far more difficult than just giving up on it yourself. If you know your friend is waiting at the corner of the road for your morning run, turning over and staying in bed means that you're letting them down not just yourself.

Allow the unexpected.

Life would be wonderful if awards went to plan, but it doesn't.

However, if you plan for the unexpected it means you won't allow these things to stand in your way.

Even with the most well thought out plan, life still happens, so there will be sometimes when you can't stick to your schedule. But if you've thought of this in advance you will be able to make allowances for this, the two useful words are **if** and **then**.

If my meeting runs late and I can't get to the gym, **then** I'll get up early tomorrow.

If I'm at a party with party food, **then** I will go for a longer walk tomorrow.

If I have to work late and can't write today, **then** I will get up an hour earlier in the morning to write my chapter.

Having this sort of plan in place means that the unexpected will not throw you off track altogether, you have considered a way around the problem, which means that you will actually do something about it and still reach your deadlines.

Use tools to help you.

There are all sorts of wonderful apps available now that can help you stick to your plan and achieve your goals, many of them can be downloaded to your smartphone or tablet so that you can keep them with you all the time.

You can get apps to help you with food journals, exercise, to-do lists, meal planning, goal setting and thousands of other things.

Have a look at the App stores – just avoid wasting all your time of the games!

You can also use tools such as spreadsheets, pedometer's, exercise programs and simple exercise equipment that you can use at home.

Just think about your resolution and decide what would help you in achieving your goals, after all why reinvent the wheel?

Visualisation.

When your resolution or goal is really challenging and life changing, you may well find that at times you doubt that you can achieve it, and that doubt will very quickly lead to a lack of confidence and failure.

But visualisation is a very useful technique and it can help you overcome your fear.

Start visualising about how you will feel when you reach your goal. After all visualising is a very positive form of daydreaming, and if you don't dream how will your dreams come true?

So start to visualise daily how you will feel when you reach your goal.

Imagine it in as much detail as you can.

If your goal is to lose weight, close your eyes and just see how you will look when you fit into those skinny jeans. Imagine how good you will feel and the admiring glances you will enjoy.

If your goal is to get fitter just close your eyes and imagine crossing the finishing line of the marathon. Imagine the surge of adrenaline, the excitement of being successful.

If your goal is to clear your debts, imagine how will feel when you don't have to worry about the bills arriving each month and your money running out before the month does.

The more you visualise something, the more real it will become, because you will be making connections in your brain for positive rather than negative thoughts.

Consequences.

The opposite side of the coin to visualisation is to accept the consequences of failing to stick to your step-by-step plan.

It's far too easy to give in, that's why so many people fail to stick to the resolutions. After all it's much easier to miss going to the gym instead of going out in the cold and wet and dark. It's far easier to have a piece of cake because everybody else is having some, or to miss doing your writing today, or to buy something you don't need and ruin your budgeting plan.

All of these things are easy, and done once in a while they will not ruin your overall plan, but if it becomes a habit and you simply give up on your plan then you become one of those failures.

So when you feel yourself slipping, and thinking one won't hurt, take the time to think about your long term goal and the damage you will do to it if you give into temptation.

Is one chocolate bar really good enough to give up on your dream of losing weight?

Is that one extra handbag in the sale really worth the debt you're keeping yourself in?

Is sitting on the sofa watching some TV really better than writing the next chapter?

Once you think about the consequences, your willpower is much more likely to come to the fore, giving you the strength to avoid temptation.

Groups and forums.

You can find a group or a forum for almost anything nowadays, and joining a group of like-minded people is an excellent way to keep you on track to reach your goal.

Not many people actually like working alone or can keep motivated without help. But joining a forum or group means the you will be with other people who have the same targets as you have and you will all be able to work together to keep each other motivated.

It also means that you won't feel alone and that you're not the only one struggling with the difficulties you find in reaching your target.

Knowing that you are not the only person in the world struggling with your particular demon is very comforting and can help renew your willpower and get you back on track with your plan.

Challenges.

Many of us like a challenge and getting other people involved is a very good and fun way to accomplish your goal.

If your goal is to eat a healthier diet then you could blog about it, challenging other people to join you, or setting a challenge at work.

Challenges are particularly useful when you have self-improvement goals such as weight loss, fitness, giving up smoking or alcohol or learning a new skill. Once this is turned into a challenge it adds impetus to the process. Not only are you doing this for yourself you are competing against others, and competition often gives you the drive to succeed.

Bite-size pieces.

As I said earlier breaking down a large goal or resolution into easier chunks will make you much more likely to succeed.

If your resolution is truly life changing it can also seem totally overwhelming, after all it's huge. And when it feels so overwhelming the natural temptation is to give in before you even start which is so why so many New Year's resolutions are ancient history by the end of January.

But once you break it down into bite-size pieces you can concentrate on each of these little chunks and they are much more manageable.

You can, indeed you should, use this technique for any of the larger tasks in life whether that is completing a degree, redecorating the house, redesigning a garden, losing weight, writing a book or fixing your finances.

As they say, the longest journey starts with a single step.

So instead of looking at the garden which is resembling the jungle, turning around, going back inside and having a coffee, look at a single shrub or a single flower bed and focus on that. Once you have dealt with that single shrub or flowerbed, you will actually have achieved something and you will feel able to move on to the next chunk, before you know where you are the jungle will have been tamed and it will look like a garden again.

If that sounds personal, it is!

My mum broke her leg few years ago and the garden was left to fend for itself for a year, by which time it was making a good attempt at turning into a jungle and it seemed totally overwhelming when I looked at the whole picture. So I just focused on one piece at a time and was pleased when that one bit was done. Then I could move on to the next bit.

Have a day off.

There is nothing wrong with having a day off, the secret is to book it as a day off.

If you plan in advance, then it is in your plan and you won't fall into the trap of just having a day off any time you feel like it. That would lead to giving up.

But if you plan your day off, you can look forward to it, you can plan what you are going to do and anticipate it.

You might want to pick a day to spend time with your family or friends.

You might want to plan a day off from your diet program so that you can enjoy a family party or celebration.

You might want to plan a day off from your fitness program so you can go out with friends for pizza and a glass of wine without feeling guilty.

Having a day off or a cheat day can stop you being overwhelmed by the task you have set yourself, after all everyone needs a break whatever it is you're doing. It means you will come back refreshed and energised, which will make you more likely to succeed in the long term.

Take a break.

This is the same as having a day off, this means not constantly thinking about your goal or resolution.

Although it's important not to lose focus, if your goal becomes the only thing you are thinking of, you will become blinkered to what is actually happening around you. This can be exhausting and you're much more likely to give up altogether.

Instead of focusing on your goal all the time, you should make some conscious choices and then relax a little, relying on yourself to create new habits and do these things automatically. This means that they will simply become part of your normal routine rather than something that you have to concentrate on at all times.

Even when you are chasing an enormous goal you still have to leave room for living.

Success breeds success.

Have you ever noticed that spending time with somebody who is negative is exhausting? They moan, and moan, and moan, and moan and after a few hours you feel absolutely miserable.

Luckily the same works the other way and if you spend your time with successful people who have a positive attitude, then that energy will rub off on you as well.

So make sure that you spend time with successful, positive people who believe in themselves and believe that they can reach their goals. You will find yourself uplifted, recharged, enthused and ready for success.

Keep a Journal.

It doesn't have to be a journal, it could be a set of photographs. The thing is that it helps you to keep a reminder of where you've come from and where you've reached.

When you're working towards a goal, there will always be times when you lose sight of your success and when you feel as if you're just not getting anywhere. That's why it is a very good idea to keep reminders of where you started and how far you have come.

Exactly how you keep these reminders will depend on your resolution or goal, you could keep notes, you could write a journal, or you could keep a series of photos that show how far you have come.

The idea is to create some kind of record that you can look at or read when you feel that you just aren't getting anywhere. A record that will remind you of your successes and give you a reason to congratulate yourself.

It will also give you the confidence and drive to continue making successful steps towards your ultimate target.

Plan to succeed.

A plan is essential if you want to succeed with your New Year's resolutions.

When you plan ahead you can anticipate the problems you will face and through doing this you can eliminate the tough choices and be more prepared to resist sudden temptations.

For instance, if your New Year's resolution is to eat more healthily, you should set time aside to plan your weekly menu. This means that you can do your grocery shopping with a list and select healthy choices. And having a plan for your meals each day, means that you can stick to your healthy eating rather than just grabbing the nearest ready meal. If possible it is even better if you can pre-prepare your meals by doing batch cooking and freezing or using a slow cooker. By doing that you will be able to have a healthy meal no matter how tired you are when you come home from work and no matter how difficult your day has been.

This system can be used for any resolution. Planning where you are going and how you are going to get there makes it much more likely that you will actually succeed. Simply relying on a vague wish is the fastest route to failure that you could find.

Set monthly goals.

If a New Year's resolution is really worth its name it will probably take a while to achieve and it can be difficult to keep your motivation going, although setting a plan and keeping a journal can help.

But it can also help if you create monthly goals. After all, a month is much more manageable than a year.

If you break your resolution into monthly segments, it means you will have a new deadline each month and that is a much more successful way of keeping you on target.

It also means that you will be able to celebrate success every month, which is very good way of keeping you motivated.

Have self-belief.

Believing in yourself is an absolute necessity if you want to succeed in your plans.

Self-doubt becomes a self-fulfilling prophecy. If you don't believe you can achieve your dreams, then you never will achieve them.

By believing that your goal is possible you will automatically improve your success rate, it will help you resist temptation because you know you can reach your goal, and your willpower will stay strong because of that belief.

Using affirmations.

Positive affirmations are a very good way of strengthening your self-belief. They help motivate you and create new pathways in your brain. Telling yourself something over and over again is like teaching yourself a new lesson.

We often experience this in a negative way. If somebody tells you over and over again that you're not clever enough, you're not pretty enough, you'll never succeed, you can't make it on your own, you will eventually believe them. It's a form of abuse that many bullies use to control other people. But from our point of view, the important lesson to learn about it is that it works. And if it can work for negative messages it can most certainly work if you continually give yourself positive messages.

You can find many affirmations in books and online, and you need to find one that suits you and that you are comfortable with. It might feel a bit unnatural or even silly at first but it's important to keep using the affirmation you have chosen, speaking the words out loud over and over, day after day, week after week until you believe it.

Here are some quotations to get you started, but do look around and find one that you are comfortable with. Of course you can use more than one or you can change your quotations as you move through your goal.

It is good to have an end to journey towards: but it is the journey that matters, in the end

Ernest Hemingway.

If you really want to live a happy life, tie it to a goal, not to people or things.

Albert Einstein.

When it's obvious that the goals cannot be reached, don't adjust the goals, adjust the action steps.

Confucius

Ask for help.

If you feel you need help in moving towards your goal, in achieving your resolution, then ask for help. None of us are superhuman, none of us can do everything on our own and none of us have to face the world alone. If you feel you are struggling, then just reach out and ask for help and advice.

You'll probably be surprised. Most people don't like to offer the help because they don't want to hurt your feelings, but they'll be there for you as soon as you ask.

Setting milestones.

I've mentioned a few times the importance of breaking a task down into smaller bite-size chunks, and of breaking a very large goal into more achievable sections, but if you have a major resolution or goal, and you know that it is going to take a considerable time to reach your final target, then it can be very useful to create a set of milestones for yourself.

For instance, your New Year's resolution may be to get on the property ladder, to buy your dream home, to study for a degree or to become financially independent.

There's no reason you shouldn't choose any of these things to be your New Year's resolution, but you're probably not going to achieve it in a single year.

So it can be very useful to break this down into a series of steps, which you will then probably break down into bite-size chunks.

Setting milestones can help you stay on track with a long-term goal, otherwise the overwhelming task that you have set yourself will probably defeat you.

Each of your milestones will be a step on the way and will help you progress towards your end goal, in fact you could look at them as mini goals.

For instance you may need to do some preparatory study and exams before you can start a degree, or you may need to work your way through a variety of properties to reach your dream home.

If you look at your ultimate goal without really taking into account these preparatory steps, you will probably give up because the overall task you have set yourself will feel unachievable.

Wishing for something is fine if you just want a lovely fantasy life, but this book is about actually getting there.

Obviously your personal milestones will depend entirely on your overall goal, your personal circumstances and your other responsibilities in life.

You should invest time and thought in this. You need to plan seriously and to be honest about the steps you need to take, and the preparation you need to do. If you are looking at a very large goal, you are planning to transform your life and this deserves your investment in planning it properly.

As you reach each milestone, you can take the time to evaluate your progress and to check that your final goal is still correct for you.

There is nothing wrong with adjusting your plan.

You will learn things as you go along and your opinions and dreams may change. There is no point sticking rigidly to a plan just because that's what you decided upon in the first place. Changing your end goal is not the same as giving up, it is adapting and growing as you learn.

Each milestone also gives you the opportunity to review what you have done so far, to accept responsibility for your actions and to correct any mistakes you may have made.

As I said, life happens and unexpected things will crop up during your journey, especially during a long journey.

You need to be able to accept this, adjust to new circumstances and set your new path if required.

You should set each milestone as a mini goal complete with its own deadlines and plan of action. Celebrate your successes along the way, they will keep you motivated and encourage you as you move forward.

When you have reached your milestone it is worth re-examining your overall goal to make sure that the details are still what you want.

As they say, Rome wasn't built in a day, so if you want to transform your life, live the dream you have dreamed, and be able to look back and say 'I did that', then plan properly, set your milestones and start your journey with that first step.

Josie Baxter

Some suggestions for your New Year's resolution.

Josie Baxter

Resolution ideas.

You probably know what you want to change in life and what your New Year's resolutions should be, but sometimes it's a bit too easy to get caught up in the fashion, the hype, in following what everybody else is doing.

But if you want to succeed in your resolution, it has to be something you actually want to do.

So I've put a few samples together to start you thinking. I'm not suggesting that you simply pick one of them out, this is not a list of the right things to do, they are there to spark ideas, to set off a train of thought, to make you think about your own goals.

So read through them and see what resonates with you, and what ideas of your own you come up with.

Health and fitness.
Lose 10 pounds by April
run ½ marathon in July.
Wear a bikini on your summer holiday.
Learn how to ride a bike.
Cut out sugar.
Eat more fruit and vegetables.
Only eat take out once a month.

Take up yoga.
Drop a dress size by March.
Take up weight training.
Go meatless at least one day a week.
Give up smoking
Give up alcohol for January
Get a six pack by Easter.
Learn to ski.
Do something that scares you every month.

Personal finance.
Become debt free by December.
Increased payments on your student loan.
Set up regular savings.
Save enough for a house deposit by December.
Set a long-term saving plan.
Cut out impulse buys.
Clear your mortgage.
Move to a better house.
Buy a newer car.
Take a second job.
Sell your unwanted stuff.

Career plans.
Submit your resume to 10 employers by 1st February.
Self-publish that book you have written.
Set a goal for your promotion.
Start that business you've always wanted.
Take professional exams.
Improve your skills.

Be in higher paid employment by December.
Move to flexible working.

Improve your skills.
Finish your degree.
Train for a new career.
Take a computer course.
Learn a foreign language.
Learn to play a musical instrument.
Become a licensed yoga instructor.
Improve your career skills to the next level.

Family goals.
Set Sunday as family time.
Visit your parents at least once a month.
Read your children a bedtime story.
Plan a monthly family night at the movies.
Play a sport with your children.
Plan experiences as a family and schedule them.
Help your children make New Year's resolutions.
Always make time for the school play.
Always make time for the sports day.
Always be there for birthday parties.

Relationship goals.
Celebrate your wedding anniversary this year.
Have a date night to at least once a week.
Send your partner flowers or a bottle of wine.
Say *I love you* more often.
Have a romantic weekend away.

End an unsuccessful relationship.
Join a dating site.
Start going on dates again.

These are just some suggestions. Your goals might involve travel, seeing the world, volunteering, improving your photography, writing your first novel, becoming more spiritual, becoming more adventurous, launching your new business, or your new invention.

Your New Year's resolution can be anything that matters to you.

In fact, that's the only rule, it has to matter to you.

If you make a New Year's resolution without really wanting it, you will almost certainly fall into that group that fails by February.

But if you make a resolution that you have really thought about, planning a change in your life that you really want to make, and if you set out a proper plan, with proper targets, realistic goals and you follow the guidelines in this book then you will have taken your first steps towards success.

And I wish you all the very best on your journey towards your new life.

May you have a very Happy, Successful and prosperous New Year.

Printed in Great Britain
by Amazon